THE GIFT
— CALLED —
LEADERSHIP

STUDY GUIDE

Cover design by: Mattie Wells
Cover photo by: Andrew van Tilborgh

ISBN: 978-1-960678-63-8   1 2 3 4 5 6 7 8 9 10

Printed in the United States of America

How the Leader's 'Presence'
Empowers Others to Succeed

THE GIFT
— CALLED —
LEADERSHIP

BARRY E. KNIGHT

STUDY GUIDE

A V A I L

CONTENTS

How the Leader's 'Presence'
Empowers Others to Succeed

THE GIFT
— CALLED —
LEADERSHIP

BARRY E KNIGHT

AWAKEN THE SPIRIT OF LEADERSHIP

The bottom line is: nations, cities, schools, communities, corporations, and organizations succeed when Leaders are in authority.

As you read
Chapter 1:
"Awaken
the Spirit of
Leadership" in
*The Gift Called
Leadership*,
review, reflect
on, and respond
to the text by
answering
the following
questions.

REVIEW, REFLECT, AND RESPOND:

What does leadership mean to you?

_____

_____

_____

_____

_____

_____

_____

What is the Spirit of Leadership? Define it in your own words.

_____

_____

_____

_____

_____

_____

_____

When does the Spirit of Leadership manifest?

_____

_____

_____

_____

_____

_____

What are the internal indicators of the Spirit of Leadership? Are all of these indicators present within your organization?

_____

_____

_____

_____

_____

_____

_____

What is your organization's global vision?

_____

_____

_____

_____

_____

_____

What are the external indicators of a Spirit of Leadership? Are you missing any of these?

_____

_____

_____

_____

_____

_____

_____

How do you serve others as a leader?

_____

_____

_____

_____

_____

_____

_____

What do you do for personal growth? How do you invest in the team's growth?

_____

_____

_____

_____

_____

_____

_____

What needs to change for the Spirit of Leadership to be present in your life and work?

_____

_____

_____

_____

_____

_____

_____

CHAPTER 2

BE SELF-AWARE AND FULLY PRESENT

By being a self-aware and fully present Leader, you begin the journey of establishing an environment where people begin to willingly trust you, trust your Leadership, and trust your ability to lead them to the vision.

REVIEW, REFLECT, AND RESPOND:

How would you define self-awareness?

_____

_____

_____

_____

_____

Do you consider yourself to be self-aware? Have you always been this way?

_____

_____

_____

_____

_____

_____

Describe a time when you or someone you've interacted with has shown no self-awareness. What was the outcome?

_____

_____

_____

_____

_____

_____

_____

How do you identify opportunities to grow?

_____

_____

_____

_____

_____

_____

_____

What are the advantages of self-awareness?

_____

_____

_____

_____

_____

_____

_____

What does being fully present mean? What needs to happen before this can take place?

_____

_____

_____

_____

_____

_____

_____

What does it mean to be "fully present with your yes"?

_____

_____

_____

_____

_____

_____

Which of the four areas of being fully present do you struggle with most? Why?

_____

_____

_____

_____

_____

_____

_____

What are the enemies of being self-aware and fully present?

_____

_____

_____

_____

_____

_____

_____

EARN THEIR TRUST, RESPECT, AND CONFIDENCE

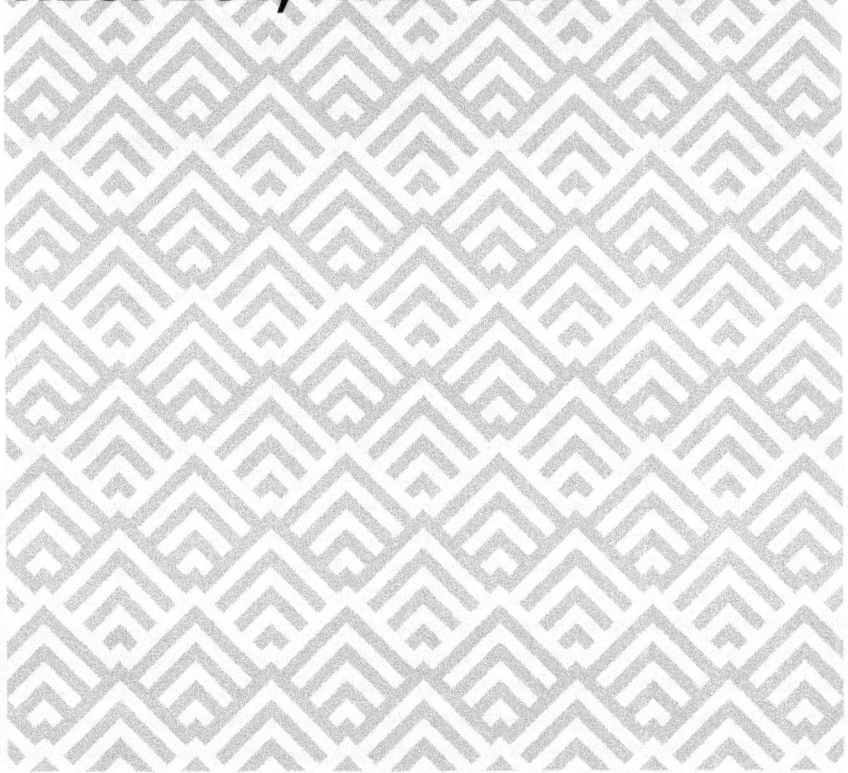

As you lead and help others succeed, you make deposits into their trust, respect, and confidence account.

READING
TIME

As you read
Chapter 3: "Earn
Their Trust,
Respect, and
Confidence" in
*The Gift Called
Leadership*,
review, reflect
on, and respond
to the text by
answering
the following
questions.

REVIEW, REFLECT, AND RESPOND:

Do you have the trust, respect, and confidence of those you lead?

_____

_____

_____

_____

How do you personally come to trust, respect, and have confidence in someone else?

_____

_____

_____

_____

_____

_____

Do you feel you are adequately answering the three questions teams ask of their leaders? Which question could you more effectively answer?

_____

_____

_____

_____

_____

_____

_____

_____

> *A double minded man is unstable in all his ways.*
>
> —James 1:8

Consider the scripture above and answer the following questions

What does this scripture reveal about being trustworthy?

_____

_____

_____

_____

_____

_____

_____

Have you ever encountered a "double-minded" person? Describe the situation.

_____

_____

_____

_____

_____

_____

_____

_____

What are the benefits of earning the trust of your team? Do you see these present within your organization currently?

_____

_____

_____

_____

_____

_____

_____

_____

_____

What are the benefits of earning respect?

_____

_____

_____

_____

_____

_____

_____

_____

_____

What are the benefits of earning the confidence of others?

_____

_____

_____

_____

_____

_____

_____

_____

CHAPTER 4

GIVE THEM SOMETHING TO BELIEVE IN

Your vision makes people better. Vision inspires people to follow.

REVIEW, REFLECT, AND RESPOND:

What vision have you given your team to look ahead to?

_____

_____

_____

_____

_____

_____

Have you effectively communicated this vision and reinforced this vision to your team? Would they agree?

_____

_____

_____

_____

_____

_____

Do you feel your team is invested in the vision? Why or why not?

_____

_____

_____

_____

_____

_____

> *And he saith unto them, Follow me, and*
> *I will make you fishers of men.*
>
> —Matthew 4:19

Consider the scripture above and answer the following questions:

What was Jesus Christ's vision?

_____

_____

_____

_____

_____

_____

How did He communicate His vision, according to this verse?

_____

_____

_____

_____

_____

_____

Seeing the vision is only the first step. What do you do to help your team believe in and subsequently work hard for the vision?

_____

_____

_____

_____

_____

_____

_____

_____

What does it mean to be a bi-dimensional leader? Are you a
bi-dimensional leader?

_____

_____

_____

_____

_____

_____

What is your S.M.A.R.T.E.S.T. Vision? Take time to craft one below.

_____

_____

_____

_____

_____

_____

_____

_____

_____

_____

_____

CHAPTER 5

LEAD THE WHOLE, NOT THE PART

Leading the whole requires a comprehensive and collaborative systems-thinking strategy that involves stakeholders.

READING TIME

As you read Chapter 5: "Lead the Whole, Not the Part" in *The Gift Called Leadership*, review, reflect on, and respond to the text by answering the following questions.

REVIEW, REFLECT, AND RESPOND:

Have you ever been part of a broken or fragmented team? What was your experience?

_____

_____

_____

_____

_____

_____

_____

_____

On a scale of one to ten (one being completely broken and ten being completely whole) how would you rate your team?

1   2   3   4   5   6   7   8   9   10

Why does your team "feeling like" and "acting as" a whole matter?

_____

_____

_____

_____

_____

_____

_____

How does a leader's ability to see the whole affect decision-making?

_____

_____

_____

_____

_____

_____

_____

What can you do as the leader to "build the whole"?

_____

_____

_____

_____

_____

_____

_____

_____

_____

When has your organization undergone major change, if ever? How did you lead your team through this transitional period?

_____

_____

_____

_____

_____

_____

_____

_____

_____

What systems and behaviors do you need to reexamine?

_____

_____

_____

_____

_____

_____

_____

_____

How does each part of your organization work together, and what problem are they working together to solve?

_____

_____

_____

_____

_____

_____

_____

_____

_____

_____

ESTABLISH THE CULTURE AND IDENTITY

Culture is who I am when I am in your world. Identity is who I am because I was exposed to your world.

READING
TIME

As you read
Chapter 6:
"Establish the
Culture and
Identity" in
*The Gift Called
Leadership*,
review, reflect
on, and respond
to the text by
answering
the following
questions.

REVIEW, REFLECT, AND RESPOND:

What is an organization's culture?

_____

_____

_____

_____

_____

How would you describe your organization's
culture? How has this changed, if at all, over
recent months and years?

_____

_____

_____

_____

_____

What is the difference between an
organization's culture and its identity?

_____

_____

_____

_____

_____

_____

How do you change or maintain a culture? What are the elements that make up an organization's culture?

_____

_____

_____

_____

_____

_____

_____

What is your organization's story? Do you tell this story enough for it to affect your culture?

_____

_____

_____

_____

_____

_____

_____

How do you ensure consistency throughout your organization? Has this ever been a challenge?

_____

_____

_____

_____

_____

_____

_____

How can you link your culture and identity to your desired outcomes?

_____

_____

_____

_____

_____

_____

_____

_____

What are the advantages of a healthy culture?

_____

_____

_____

_____

_____

_____

What is your ideal organizational identity?

_____

_____

_____

_____

_____

_____

CHAPTER 7

PRACTICE GLOBAL AWARENESS

As you learn to engage, inspire, and empower the people you lead and serve more effectively, you begin to see two worlds—yours and theirs—emerging as one.

As you read
Chapter 7:
"Practice Global
Awareness" in
*The Gift Called
Leadership*,
review, reflect
on, and respond
to the text by
answering
the following
questions.

REVIEW, REFLECT, AND RESPOND:

What is global awareness in your own words?

_____

_____

_____

_____

_____

_____

_____

Do you consider yourself to be globally
aware? Why or why not?

_____

_____

_____

_____

_____

_____

_____

How do you think better global awareness
benefits your organization?

_____

_____

_____

_____

_____

_____

What are the ten states of global awareness? Which of these are you missing?

1) _____

2) _____

3) _____

4) _____

5) _____

6) _____

7) _____

8) _____

9) _____

10) _____

_____

_____

Have you ever struggled with active listening?

_____

_____

_____

_____

_____

_____

_____

Briefly describe the differences between superficial listening, deep listening, and spirit listening.

_____

_____

_____

_____

_____

_____

_____

_____

_____

What are the differences between the state of patience and the state of peace?

_____

_____

_____

_____

_____

_____

_____

What does it mean to lead from the state of hope and faith? Do you do this?

_____

_____

_____

_____

_____

_____

_____

_____

CHAPTER 8

SPEAK LIFE

Speaking life gives energy, reproduces success, empowers others to grow, and helps teams respond to change.

REVIEW, REFLECT, AND RESPOND:

What does it mean to speak life?

_____

_____

_____

_____

_____

_____

_____

How do you speak life into others through your life and leadership?

_____

_____

_____

_____

_____

_____

_____

How can you speak life both into the present and future? What does this mean?

_____

_____

_____

_____

_____

_____

_____

Has a leader ever spoken life into you? Who and when was it? How did it make you feel?

_____

_____

_____

_____

_____

_____

_____

What are "power words"? Do you use these?

_____

_____

_____

_____

_____

_____

What are "presenting questions"? What are the advantages of these types of questions?

_____

_____

_____

_____

_____

_____

_____

When should you utilize presenting questions in your leadership?

_____

_____

_____

_____

_____

_____

_____

Describe the differences between your trust and your promise.

_____

_____

_____

_____

_____

_____

How can you be more intentional in speaking life into your team and organization?

_____

_____

_____

_____

_____

_____

_____

CHAPTER 9

RAISE OTHER LEADERS

You are here to increase their performance. You lead them so you can help them function and collaborate and work together more cohesively.

As you read Chapter 9: "Raise Other Leaders" in *The Gift Called Leadership*, review, reflect on, and respond to the text by answering the following questions.

REVIEW, REFLECT, AND RESPOND:

Who shares your burden of leadership?
What are the five burdens of leadership?

_____

_____

_____

1) _____

_____

2) _____

_____

3) _____

_____

4) _____

_____

5) _____

_____

If you were to leave your position today, who would be your successor and why? What can you do to prepare them for a possible succession?

_____

_____

_____

_____

_____

_____

_____

_____

What leadership qualities do you see in those you lead? In whom do you see them?

_____

_____

_____

_____

_____

_____

_____

_____

Have you ever been intimidated by another leader? Describe the situation. What intimidated you? How did you overcome this?

_____

_____

_____

_____

_____

_____

_____

What needs to change in order for you to be considered a coaching leader?

_____

_____

_____

_____

_____

_____

_____

_____

_____

_____

_____

Are you aware of the goals your team is currently working toward on an individual level? Why or why not?

_____

_____

_____

_____

_____

_____

_____

_____

How can you be more present and helpful in raising up and challenging your team?

_____

_____

_____

_____

_____

_____

_____

_____

www.ingramcontent.com/pod-product-compliance
Lightning Source LLC
Chambersburg PA
CBHW070051100426
42734CB00040B/2986